For my sister, Miranda
IO

For Caroline and John
CR

Haiku is an ancient form of Japanese poetry. Each poem is three lines long.
The first and final lines have five syllables and the middle line has seven.
Haiku were traditionally written to celebrate the natural world.

CATERPILLAR BOOKS
An imprint of the Little Tiger Group
1 Coda Studios, 189 Munster Road, London SW6 6AW
www.littletiger.co.uk • First published in Great Britain 2019
This edition published 2020
Text by Isabel Otter
Text copyright © Caterpillar Books Ltd. 2019
Illustrations copyright © Clover Robin 2019
All rights reserved • ISBN: 978-1-83891-039-6
Printed in China • CPB/1800/1452/0720
2 4 6 8 10 9 7 5 3 1

Animal partnerships in the wild

Together

LiTTLE TiGER

LONDON

Written by

Isabel Otter

Illustrated by

Clover Robin

A vast migration.
Cranes take turns to lead their flock:
The feathered arrow.

Cranes migrate for thousands of miles.
When the leader of the group tires,
it drops back, and another crane
swoops in to take its place.

Running with the pack.
These hunters work together;
Each wolf knows its place.

*Wolves live in packs with strong
social bonds and ranking systems.*

Danger in the air...
Her stamping hooves and whistles
Alert the chamois.

Female chamois live in herds with their young. One member of the herd is always on the lookout for predators.

In the ocean deep,
Whales glide in sweeping circles
To mesmerise prey.

Pilot whales work together to feed, using clicks and whistles to communicate.

Hitch a ride with shark,
Share his food and keep him clean.
Happy arrangement.

The remora fish attach themselves to sharks using suckers. They nibble parasites on the shark's skin and benefit from a free lift.

Goby make their home
Among the waving tendrils;
Sheltered and secure.

Snakelocks anemones protect goby fish from predators with stinging tentacles. Goby fish keep the anemones clean.

The badger follows
The twittering sing-song trail
Leading to honey.

The honey badger pulls down the
hive, and shares the honeycomb
with the honey guide bird.

A crocodile smiles.
Plover hops in for a snack,
Pecking the fangs clean.

Plover birds eat leftovers from the mouths of crocodiles. In return, the crocodiles get their teeth cleaned!

Marching one by one,
Their bond will last a lifetime.
Herd and family.

Elephants are very loyal to their herd and always keep pace with the slowest member.

Free grooming service
For gracious, stately giraffes.
Peck, peck, busy birds.

Oxpecker birds perch on the backs
of giraffes, feeding on their fleas
and providing pest control.

Two unlikely friends
Listening and keeping watch.
Safer together.

Zebras have a good sense of smell and hearing, but poor sight. Ostriches have great sight, but can't smell or hear well. They alert each other to danger.

The flock soars downwards.
Moonlight glimmers on the lake;
Journey at an end.

*These cranes have flown thousands
of miles over land and sea to reach
their winter feeding grounds.*